Mastering Metaverse Game Development:

Building Immersive Worlds

Georgeann J.

Table of Contents:

Chapter 1: Introduction to the Metaverse

Understanding the Metaverse Concept

In recent years, the term "Metaverse" has taken the tech world by storm. It has become a buzzword in discussions about the future of technology, gaming, and virtual reality. But what exactly is the Metaverse, and why is it such a compelling concept?

Defining the Metaverse

The Metaverse is a virtual universe, a collective digital space that encompasses a vast, interconnected network of augmented reality (AR) and virtual reality (VR) environments, applications, and users. In essence, it is a convergence of physical and digital realities, creating an immersive, shared, and persistent digital realm.

A Brief History

The concept of the Metaverse can be traced back to science fiction literature, particularly Neal Stephenson's 1992 novel "Snow Crash," which described a virtual reality-based successor to the internet called the "Metaverse." Since then, the idea has captured the imagination of technologists, gamers, and futurists.

Key Characteristics of the Metaverse

Interconnectivity:

The Metaverse is not limited to a single virtual world; it consists of many interconnected digital spaces. These spaces can be accessed seamlessly, allowing users to move from one environment to another without barriers.

User-Generated Content:

In the Metaverse, users have the power to create and modify their environments, objects, and experiences. This user-generated content (UGC) is a fundamental aspect of the Metaverse, enabling creativity and customization.

Persistence:

Unlike traditional online games or virtual experiences, the Metaverse is always "on." It doesn't reset, and it continues to exist even when users log out. This persistence creates a sense of a living, breathing world.

Economy:

The Metaverse often has its economy, with digital assets and currencies. Blockchain technology plays a significant role in ensuring ownership and scarcity of digital items through non-fungible tokens (NFTs) and smart contracts.

Applications Beyond Gaming

While gaming is a prominent part of the Metaverse, its potential extends far beyond entertainment. The Metaverse has applications in education, business collaboration, social interaction, healthcare, and more. It serves as a versatile platform for a wide range of human activities.

The Promise and Challenges

The Metaverse promises a new era of connectivity and digital experiences. However, it also poses challenges related to privacy, security, governance, and accessibility. Striking the right balance between innovation and protection will be a crucial aspect of its development.

In this book, we will delve deeper into the Metaverse's various facets, exploring the technologies that power it, the opportunities it presents, and the challenges it faces. Whether you're a game developer, a tech enthusiast, or simply curious about the future of digital interaction, this book will be your guide to understanding and navigating the exciting realm of the Metaverse.

The Evolution of Virtual Worlds

Virtual worlds have come a long way since their inception, evolving from rudimentary text-based environments to immersive, visually stunning universes. This evolution has been driven by technological advancements, changing user expectations, and the growing importance of virtual spaces in various aspects of our lives.

Text-Based MUDs (Multi-User Dungeons):

The earliest virtual worlds can be traced back to the 1970s with text-based MUDs. These were essentially interactive stories where players typed commands to navigate and interact with a textual environment. While primitive by today's standards, they laid the foundation for virtual world development.

Graphical MMORPGs (Massively Multiplayer Online Role-Playing Games):

The 1990s saw the emergence of graphical MMORPGs like Ultima Online and EverQuest. These games introduced 2D and later 3D graphics, allowing players to explore expansive, persistent virtual worlds. Social interaction became a key aspect, with players forming communities and guilds.

Second Life and the Metaverse Concept:

In the early 2000s, Second Life popularized the concept of virtual worlds as social platforms. Users could create and customize their avatars, build virtual property, and engage in various activities. This era marked the beginning of the idea of a "metaverse" where people could live, work, and socialize.

Virtual Reality (VR) and Augmented Reality (AR):

The advent of VR and AR technologies in the 2010s brought a new dimension to virtual worlds. VR headsets enabled immersive experiences, while AR integrated virtual elements into the real world. Games like "Pokemon Go" showcased the potential of AR, while VR platforms like Oculus Rift and HTC Vive pushed the boundaries of immersion.

Blockchain and NFTs:

In recent years, blockchain technology and non-fungible tokens (NFTs) have gained prominence in virtual worlds. These technologies enable ownership of virtual assets and the creation of decentralized virtual spaces. Projects like Decentraland and The Sandbox allow users to buy, sell, and build on virtual land using blockchain technology.

Emerging Applications:

Beyond gaming and social interaction, virtual worlds are finding applications in education, training, and remote work. Virtual classrooms, corporate meeting spaces, and virtual events have become more common, especially in response to the COVID-19 pandemic.

Interoperability and the Metaverse Vision:

A key trend is the push for interoperability between virtual worlds, fostering the creation of a metaverse where users can seamlessly move between different virtual spaces using a single avatar or identity. Tech giants like Facebook (now Meta) are investing heavily in realizing this vision.

The evolution of virtual worlds continues to be shaped by advancements in technology and the changing needs and desires of users. As the lines between the physical and virtual worlds blur, virtual environments are poised to become an integral part of our future, impacting how we socialize, work, learn, and create. The concept of the metaverse remains at the forefront of this evolution, promising a connected and immersive digital universe that transcends today's boundaries.

Metaverse Opportunities in Game Development

The concept of the metaverse has gained significant attention in recent years, and it presents numerous opportunities in the field of game development. The metaverse is essentially a virtual universe where users can interact with each other and digital environments in real time. Here are some of the key opportunities it offers to game developers:

Immersive Gaming Experiences:

The metaverse allows for the creation of highly immersive gaming environments that go beyond traditional single-player or multiplayer experiences. Players can engage in persistent, interconnected worlds that offer rich storytelling and gameplay.

Cross-Platform Play:

With the metaverse, developers can create games that are accessible on various devices, from VR headsets to smartphones and PCs. This enables a wider audience to join the same gaming universe regardless of their preferred platform.

User-Generated Content:

Game developers can empower players to contribute to the metaverse by creating their content, such as in-game items, characters, or even entire worlds. This not only enhances player engagement but also provides opportunities for user-generated economies.

Economic Opportunities:

The metaverse can function as a digital marketplace where in-game assets can be bought, sold, and traded using blockchain technology. Developers can monetize their creations through asset sales, and players can potentially earn real-world income.

Social Interactions:

Game developers can leverage the metaverse to create social spaces where players can meet, interact, and collaborate. These spaces can host virtual events, concerts, or conferences, expanding the scope of gaming experiences.

Persistent Worlds:

In traditional games, progress is often limited to a single session. In the metaverse, game worlds can be persistent, and evolving. This offers opportunities for long-term engagement and evolving storylines.

Data and Analytics:

The metaverse generates a wealth of data on player behavior and interactions. Game developers can use this data to refine their games, personalize experiences, and optimize monetization strategies.

Collaborations:

Developers can collaborate with other creators and companies within the metaverse, leading to unique crossover events and experiences that benefit both parties.

AI Integration:

Integrating AI into the metaverse can enhance the gaming experience by creating dynamic and responsive environments, as well as providing personalized challenges and content.

Accessibility:

The metaverse can be designed to accommodate individuals with disabilities, promoting inclusivity and reaching a broader audience.

In conclusion, the metaverse opens up a new frontier for game developers, offering the potential for innovative and expansive gaming experiences. However, it also comes with challenges such as privacy concerns, technical hurdles, and the need for robust infrastructure. As the metaverse continues to develop, those in the game development industry will have the opportunity to shape its future and create groundbreaking experiences for players worldwide

Chapter 2: Metaverse Technologies

In recent years, the concept of the metaverse has evolved from science fiction into a tangible and transformative reality. Metaverse technologies are ushering in a new era of digital interconnectedness, where virtual worlds, augmented reality, and immersive experiences converge to create a vast and interconnected digital universe. This technological frontier promises to revolutionize how we work, play, socialize, and even define our identities. In this exploration, we will delve into the exciting realm of metaverse technologies, examining their origins, current capabilities, and the profound impact they are poised to have on our lives. Welcome to the metaverse, where the boundaries between the physical and digital realms blur, and the possibilities are as limitless as our imagination.

Blockchain and NFTs

NFTs, or Non-Fungible Tokens, are a type of digital asset that represents ownership or proof of authenticity of a unique item or piece of content using blockchain technology. Unlike cryptocurrencies such as Bitcoin or Ethereum, NFTs are indivisible and cannot be exchanged on a one-to-one basis because each NFT has a distinct value and distinct characteristics.

Blockchain, on the other hand, is a decentralized and distributed digital ledger technology that underpins many cryptocurrencies and NFTs. It consists of a chain of blocks, each containing a record of transactions. These blocks are linked together using cryptography, making them extremely secure and tamper-resistant.

When it comes to NFTs and blockchain, there are a few key points to consider:

Ownership and Provenance: NFTs use blockchain to establish and verify ownership of digital items, such as digital art, music, collectibles, or virtual real estate. This provides a transparent and immutable record of ownership history, ensuring authenticity and provenance.

Scarcity and Rarity:

NFTs can create scarcity in the digital realm by limiting the number of tokens representing a particular item. This rarity often drives their value, as collectors are willing to pay for unique or limited-edition digital assets.

Smart Contracts:

Many NFTs are governed by smart contracts, which are self-executing agreements with predefined rules. These contracts can automate processes like royalties for creators each time an NFT is resold, providing ongoing income to artists and content creators.

Interoperability:

Some NFTs are designed to be interoperable across different virtual worlds and platforms, allowing users to use their digital assets in various online ecosystems.

Environmental Concerns:

NFTs and blockchains have faced criticism for their energy consumption, particularly proof-of-work blockchains like Ethereum. Efforts are underway to mitigate these concerns through more eco-friendly blockchain technologies.

In summary, NFTs leverage blockchain technology to create unique, verifiable digital assets with ownership rights. They have gained significant attention in the world of art, entertainment, and collectibles but also come with challenges related to energy consumption and market volatility.

Augmented Reality (AR) and Virtual Reality (VR)

Augmented Reality (AR) and Virtual Reality (VR) are two immersive technologies that have gained significant attention and applications in various fields. While they share similarities in providing immersive experiences, they differ in their core principles and applications.

Augmented Reality (AR):

AR is a technology that blends digital content with the real world. It overlays computer-generated images, sounds, or data onto the user's view of the physical environment, typically through a smartphone, tablet, or AR headset. AR enhances the user's perception of reality by adding virtual elements to it. Some key points about AR include:

Applications:

AR has found applications in a wide range of industries, including gaming, education, healthcare, marketing, and navigation. Popular examples include Pokémon Go, which blends virtual creatures with the real world, and

AR navigation apps that provide real-time directions.

Interaction:

AR allows users to interact with both the real and virtual worlds simultaneously. Users can manipulate virtual objects or access digital information while still being aware of their physical surroundings.

Devices:

AR experiences can be accessed on various devices, from smartphones and tablets to dedicated AR headsets like Microsoft HoloLens and Google Glass.

Practical Uses:

In industry and healthcare, AR is used for training, maintenance, and surgery planning. In marketing, it enhances product visualization, and in education, it makes learning more engaging.

Virtual Reality (VR):

VR creates a fully immersive digital environment that isolates users from the physical world. It typically involves wearing a VR headset that covers the user's vision entirely, transporting them to a computer-generated world. Some key aspects of VR are:

Immersive Environment:

VR aims to provide a complete sense of presence in a virtual world, shutting out the real surroundings entirely. This is achieved through high-quality graphics, spatial audio, and motion tracking.

Applications:

VR has been widely used in gaming, where users can be fully immersed in virtual game worlds. However, it extends beyond gaming to applications like virtual tours, therapy, architectural design, and remote collaboration.

Interaction:

Users in VR can interact with the virtual environment using motion controllers, hand gestures, or even full-body tracking, enabling a high degree of immersion and interactivity.

Devices:
VR headsets come in various forms, from tethered systems like the Oculus Rift to standalone devices like the Oculus Quest and mobile VR using smartphones.

Training and Simulation:
VR is extensively used for training simulations in fields such as aviation, military, and healthcare, where the risk and cost of real-world training are prohibitive.

In summary, AR enhances the real world by adding digital elements, whereas VR immerses users entirely into a computer-generated environment. Both technologies have transformative potential in various domains, and their continued development promises exciting opportunities for entertainment, education, training, and beyond. The choice between AR and VR depends on the specific use case and the desired level of immersion.

Spatial Computing

Spatial computing refers to a revolutionary technology that blends the physical and digital worlds seamlessly, enhancing our interaction with information and our surroundings. It's achieved through the integration of various technologies like augmented reality (AR), virtual reality (VR), mixed reality (MR), and sensor systems.

In spatial computing, digital information is no longer confined to screens or devices; it's mapped onto the physical environment. This allows users to engage with digital content in a more natural and immersive way. For instance, AR glasses can overlay digital data onto your field of vision, providing contextually relevant information as you navigate the real world.

Spatial computing has the potential to transform numerous industries. In healthcare, it can assist surgeons with augmented visualizations during complex procedures. In education, it can create immersive learning environments. Architects and engineers can use it for better design visualization, and the gaming industry is pushing the boundaries of immersive experiences.

One of the key drivers behind spatial computing's growth is its ability to enhance human-computer interaction. By utilizing gestures, voice commands, and even eye tracking, users can interact with digital content effortlessly. This shift from traditional input methods like keyboards and mice to more intuitive interfaces has the potential to make technology more accessible to a broader range of people.

However, challenges such as privacy concerns, hardware limitations, and the need for robust software ecosystems must be addressed for spatial computing to reach its full potential. As the technology continues to evolve, it promises to reshape how we work, learn, entertain ourselves, and connect with the world around us, ushering in a new era of computing

Interoperability and Standards

Interoperability and standards are crucial concepts in the world of technology and information systems.

Interoperability refers to the ability of different systems or components to work together seamlessly, allowing them to exchange data and functionality effectively. It ensures that diverse technologies, platforms, and applications can communicate and function harmoniously. This is especially important in today's interconnected world, where various devices and software need to collaborate to provide a cohesive user experience.

Standards play a fundamental role in achieving interoperability. They are established sets of rules, protocols, or specifications that define how different elements should behave or interact. These standards create a common language for technology, enabling compatibility and cooperation across a wide range of systems and devices.

For instance, the Internet itself relies on a multitude of standards, such as HTTP for web communication and TCP/IP for data transmission. These standards ensure that websites, servers, and browsers from different vendors can work together seamlessly.

In the healthcare sector, interoperability and standards are essential for securely sharing patient data between different medical systems. This not only improves patient care but also streamlines administrative processes.

In the context of smart homes, interoperability allows various devices like thermostats, lights, and voice assistants to communicate and respond to user commands, enhancing convenience and energy efficiency.

However, achieving interoperability is not always straightforward. It requires ongoing collaboration among industry stakeholders, consensus on standards, and adherence to those standards during product development. Additionally, technology evolves rapidly, leading to the need for updated standards to keep pace with innovation.

In conclusion, interoperability and standards are the backbone of modern technology ecosystems. They enable diverse systems to work together cohesively, facilitating innovation, efficiency, and seamless user experiences across various domains. As technology continues to advance, the importance of interoperability and adherence to standards will only grow.

Chapter 3: Designing the Metaverse Game

Conceptualizing Your Metaverse Game

The concept of a metaverse game represents a fusion of virtual reality, augmented reality, and online multiplayer, creating a digital universe where players can interact, explore, and create. To embark on the journey of conceptualizing your metaverse game, you must consider several essential factors:

Vision and Theme:

Start by defining the overarching vision for your metaverse game. What is the core theme or narrative that will immerse players in this interconnected digital realm? Whether it's a sci-fi adventure, a fantasy world, or a virtual representation of the real world, a clear vision will guide your game's development.

Platform and Technology:

Determine the technology stack and platforms your metaverse game will be built upon. Will it be primarily virtual reality (VR), augmented reality (AR), or a combination of both? The choice of technology will influence the user experience and the devices your game can run on.

World Design:

Develop a detailed world design. Consider the geography,

architecture, and ecosystem of your metaverse. Will it be a seamless, open world, or consist of interconnected zones? Pay attention to the aesthetics, as visuals play a crucial role in immersion.

Interactivity:

Define the level of interactivity and user agency within your metaverse. Will players be passive observers, explorers, or active participants shaping the world? Incorporate mechanics for social interaction, exploration, and problem-solving to engage players.

Economy and Ownership:

Explore the concept of digital ownership and economies within your metaverse. Will players be able to own virtual assets, trade them, or even create content within the game? Blockchain and NFTs (Non-Fungible Tokens) may be considered to facilitate ownership.

Social Dynamics:

Think about how social dynamics will operate in your metaverse. Will there be a system for players to form communities, alliances, or engage in commerce? Consider the moderation and governance mechanisms to ensure a positive social environment.

Monetization Model:

Decide on your game's monetization strategy. This could include subscription models, in-game purchases, or even unique monetization approaches like virtual real estate sales or digital event sponsorships.

Data Privacy and Security:

Given the vast amount of user data involved, prioritize robust data privacy and security measures to protect players' information and ensure a safe gaming environment.

Scalability:

Plan for scalability from the start. Metaverse games can attract large user bases, so your infrastructure should be able to handle growing demand without compromising performance.

User Feedback and Iteration:

Be prepared to continually gather user feedback and iterate on your metaverse game. The digital world is ever-evolving, and player input can guide improvements and new features.

Legal and Ethical Considerations:

Consult legal experts to navigate the complex legal and ethical aspects of metaverse game development, including intellectual property rights, user-generated content, and virtual asset ownership.

Community Building:

Start building a community around your metaverse game early on. Engage with potential players, create anticipation, and involve the community in shaping the game's development.

Conceptualizing a metaverse game is a monumental undertaking that requires a combination of creative vision, technical

Storytelling in a Persistent Universe

Storytelling within the realm of Metaverse programming represents a captivating fusion of technology and creativity. In this innovative space, storytelling transcends traditional narratives, giving rise to dynamic, ever-evolving experiences for participants. Here's a glimpse into how storytelling thrives in such an environment:

Dynamic Narrative Structures:

Metaverse programming allows for dynamic narrative structures, where stories adapt and evolve based on user interactions, choices, and the ever-changing virtual world. This means that each user's experience can be unique, creating a more engaging and personalized storytelling experience.

User Agency:

Participants in a persistent universe have agency over their actions and decisions, influencing the direction of the story. This interactivity is a fundamental aspect of Metaverse storytelling, as users become active participants rather than passive observers.

Emergent Storytelling:

In this environment, stories can emerge organically from user interactions. A simple action by one user can have a ripple effect, leading to unforeseen narrative developments. This unpredictability adds excitement and novelty to the storytelling experience.

Collaborative Storytelling:

Metaverse programming allows for collaborative storytelling, where users can co-create narratives with others in real time. This collaborative element fosters social connections and shared experiences, making the storytelling richer and more immersive.

Persistent World:
The Metaverse offers a persistent world where stories can unfold over extended periods, sometimes even spanning years. This long-term storytelling enables deep character development and intricate plotlines, keeping users engaged for the long haul.

Integration of AI and NPCs:
Artificial intelligence and non-playable characters (NPCs) play crucial roles in Metaverse storytelling. AI can dynamically adapt story elements based on user behavior, while NPCs can

serve as catalysts for quests, conflicts, or allies, enhancing the depth of the narrative.

User-Generated Content:

Metaverse programming often encourages user-generated content, allowing users to create and share their stories within the virtual world. This democratization of storytelling empowers users to shape the universe according to their imagination.

Economic Systems:

Some Metaverse environments incorporate economic systems where users can trade, buy, or sell virtual assets. These systems can be integrated into storytelling, creating economic storylines and incentives for users to engage with the narrative.

Cross-Platform Experiences:

Metaverse storytelling can extend beyond a single platform or device, enabling users to access and continue their stories seamlessly across various virtual spaces and devices, enhancing accessibility and convenience.

Ethical Considerations:

As Metaverse storytelling blurs the line between reality and the virtual world, ethical considerations regarding user privacy, data security, and content moderation become paramount, ensuring a safe and enjoyable experience for all participants.

In conclusion, storytelling in a Persistent Universe within the Metaverse programming landscape is a dynamic and immersive journey where creativity knows no bounds. It offers unprecedented opportunities for users to shape, participate in, and co-create narratives, making it a frontier where technology and storytelling merge to redefine the way we engage with stories.

Creating Engaging Gameplay Mechanics

Creating engaging gameplay mechanics in the metaverse involves blending virtual reality, augmented reality, and traditional gaming elements to provide a seamless and immersive experience. Here are key considerations for achieving this:

Immersive Environments:

Design rich and visually captivating virtual worlds that encourage exploration.
Implement realistic physics and spatial audio to enhance immersion.
Use AI-driven NPCs and dynamic events to create a living, breathing world.
Interactivity:

Enable natural interactions using gesture controls, voice commands, or haptic feedback.
Incorporate responsive environments that react to player actions, such as destructible

objects or dynamic weather systems.
Social Integration:

Facilitate real-time multiplayer interactions for collaborative or competitive gameplay.
Encourage social bonding through avatars, customizable identities, and in-game chat systems.

Storytelling:
Develop compelling narratives that adapt based on player choices, creating a personalized experience.
Implement non-linear storytelling techniques to maintain player engagement.

Gamification:

Reward players for achievements and progression within the metaverse.
Utilize in-game currency and items for customization and trade, fostering an in-game economy.

Cross-Platform Accessibility:

Ensure that the metaverse is accessible across various devices, including VR headsets, smartphones, and PCs, to widen the player base.

User-Generated Content:

Empower players to create and share their content within the metaverse.
Implement user-generated worlds, items, or quests to increase community engagement.

Dynamic Challenges:

Incorporate challenges that adapt to player skill levels, keeping the experience challenging yet enjoyable.

Use procedural generation to create endless possibilities in quests and environments.

Continuous Updates:

Regularly release new content, features, and improvements to keep the metaverse fresh and exciting.

Listen to player feedback and iterate on gameplay mechanics accordingly.

Ethical Considerations:

Ensure player safety and data privacy.

Prevent addiction and promote responsible gaming within the metaverse.

Creating engaging gameplay mechanics in the metaverse is a dynamic process that requires a deep understanding of technology, player psychology, and storytelling. By combining these elements, developers can create a metaverse that offers players a truly immersive and captivating gaming experience.

Chapter 4:
Metaverse Game Engines

A metaverse game engine is a specialized software framework or platform designed for creating and running virtual worlds, games, or experiences within a metaverse. These engines are responsible for rendering graphics, handling physics, managing player interactions, and enabling the creation of immersive virtual environments where users can interact and socialize.

Choosing the Right Engine

Choosing the right engine is a critical decision in various contexts, from selecting a car engine to picking the appropriate search engine for a web project. The process involves careful consideration of several key factors:

Purpose and Application:

Start by defining the purpose of the engine. Is it for transportation, power generation, or something else? Understanding the primary application helps narrow down the options.

Power and Performance:

Consider the power output required for the intended task. Engines come in various sizes and power ratings, so choose one that matches the performance needs.

Fuel Type:

Determine the type of fuel the engine will use, such as gasoline, diesel, electric, or alternative fuels like natural gas or hydrogen. Fuel availability and cost are crucial factors.

Efficiency:

Efficiency is vital to minimize operating costs and environmental impact. Look for engines with good fuel efficiency or energy conversion rates.

Environmental Impact:

Evaluate the engine's emissions and environmental impact. Many regions have regulations on emissions, so compliance is crucial.

Maintenance and Reliability:

Assess the engine's maintenance requirements and reliability. Some engines may require more frequent servicing than others, impacting downtime and costs.

Size and Space:

Consider the physical dimensions of the engine and ensure it fits the available space in your application, whether it's a vehicle, machinery, or a power plant.

Cost:

Budget constraints are essential. Determine the initial purchase cost and ongoing operational expenses, including fuel and maintenance.

Brand and Reputation:

Research the reputation of engine manufacturers. Well-established brands often offer better support and parts availability.

Future Compatibility:

Think about long-term compatibility with your project's goals. Will the chosen engine accommodate potential future upgrades or modifications?

Noise and Vibration:

For applications where noise and vibration are critical, select an engine that meets the required noise and vibration standards.

Warranty and Support:

Look for engines that come with a warranty and good customer support. This can save you money and hassle in case of unexpected issues.

Resale Value:

If applicable, consider the resale value of the engine. Some brands or types of engines hold their value better than others.

Reviews and Recommendations:

Seek out reviews and recommendations from experts and other users who have experience with the specific engine you're considering.

Regulatory Compliance:

Ensure that the engine complies with local and international regulations and safety standards.

Technology and Innovation:

Stay informed about the latest engine technologies and innovations that could improve efficiency and performance.

Choosing the right engine involves a comprehensive assessment of your specific needs and circumstances. It's a decision that should not be rushed, as making the right choice can significantly impact performance, costs, and the overall success of your project or vehicle.

Integrating AR, VR, and Mixed Reality

Integrating Augmented Reality (AR), Virtual Reality (VR), and Mixed Reality (MR) technologies offers a powerful way to reshape how we interact with the digital world and our physical surroundings. Here's an overview of these technologies and their integration:

Augmented Reality (AR):

AR enhances the real world by overlaying digital information or objects onto our physical environment. This can be achieved through smartphones, smart glasses, or headsets. AR is extensively used in industries like gaming (e.g., Pokémon Go), retail (virtual try-ons), and education (interactive learning experiences).

Virtual Reality (VR):

VR immerses users in a completely digital environment, typically through headsets that block out the real world.

VR finds applications in gaming, training simulations (e.g., flight simulators), and healthcare (pain management and therapy).

Mixed Reality (MR):

MR combines elements of both AR and VR, allowing digital objects to interact with the real world and vice versa. Users can interact with these digital elements seamlessly.

Microsoft's HoloLens is a prominent example of MR technology, used in areas like architecture (virtual building design) and remote collaboration

(virtual meetings with shared 3D models).
Integration of AR, VR, and MR:

a. Immersive Training and Education:

- Blend VR for immersive simulations with AR for real-time guidance or additional information. For instance, medical students can practice surgeries in VR while receiving AR prompts on their progress.

b. Enhanced Customer Experiences:

- Retailers can combine AR for virtual try-ons with VR for immersive shopping experiences, allowing customers to explore a virtual store and try products before purchasing.

c. Collaboration and Remote Work:

- MR enables teams to collaborate in a shared virtual environment while having access to real-world data via AR. This is especially beneficial for geographically dispersed teams.

d. Healthcare and Therapy:

- VR can be integrated with AR to create more effective therapy sessions, such as helping patients confront phobias by gradually introducing AR elements into their real environment.

e. Architecture and Design:

- Architects and designers can use MR to visualize and interact with 3D models of buildings in real-world settings, making the design and planning process more intuitive.

f. Gaming and Entertainment:

- Games can incorporate elements of both AR and VR, creating immersive gameplay experiences that bridge the gap between the digital and physical worlds.

g. Navigation and Wayfinding:

- AR can provide real-time navigation cues and information overlaid onto the user's field of view, making navigation more intuitive and safe.

Challenges:

Hardware limitations:
Integration requires compatible devices, and cost can be a barrier for some users.

Content creation:
Developing high-quality AR, VR, and MR content can be resource-intensive.

Privacy and security:
The collection of real-world data for AR and MR raises concerns about privacy and data security.

User acceptance:
Widespread adoption depends on user comfort and acceptance of these technologies.

The integration of AR, VR, and MR has the potential to revolutionize various industries by creating more immersive and interactive experiences. As technology advances and becomes more accessible, we can expect to see even more innovative applications and solutions emerge

World-Building Tools and Techniques

World-building is a crucial aspect of creating immersive fictional worlds, whether for literature, film, video games, or other forms of storytelling. Here, we'll explore some essential tools and techniques to craft rich and believable worlds:

Establish a Strong Foundation:

Start with a clear vision of your world's core elements, such as its setting, period, and key cultural or technological aspects. Decide whether your world is fantastical, futuristic, historical, or a unique blend.

Map and Geography:

Create detailed maps to visualize your world's geography. Consider how climate, terrain, and natural resources impact societies, trade routes, and conflicts.

Cultural Anthropology:

Develop the cultures and societies that inhabit your world. Consider their beliefs, traditions, languages, and values. How do these factors influence their daily lives and interactions?

History and Lore:

Craft a compelling history for your world, including significant events, legends, and myths. This backstory adds depth and authenticity to your world.

Technology and Magic Systems:

Define the level of technology or the presence of magic in your world. Establish rules and limitations to maintain consistency and prevent plot holes.

Economy and Trade:

Explore the economic systems, currencies, and trade networks within your world. Understand how resources flow and how wealth is distributed.

Politics and Power Structures:

Create governments, factions, and power dynamics. Think about how they interact and the impact they have on your story's plot and characters.

Flora and Fauna:

Populate your world with diverse and unique plant and animal life. Consider how these species fit into the ecosystem and interact with the inhabitants.

Religions and Belief Systems:

Develop religions or belief systems that shape your characters' worldviews. These can be sources of conflict, inspiration, or unity.

Character-Centric

World-Building:

Approach world-building from the perspective of your characters. How do they experience and interact with the world around them? Their perspectives can reveal details organically.

Show, Don't Tell:

Rather than info-dumping, reveal aspects of your world through character actions, dialogues, and gradual exposition. This engages readers/viewers and avoids overwhelming them with information.

Consistency and Rules:

Maintain consistency in the rules and logic of your world. Deviations should have explanations within the context of your established world-building.

Feedback and Iteration:

Seek feedback from others to ensure your world-building resonates and remains engaging. Be open to revising and refining your world as your story evolves.

Research and Inspiration:

Draw inspiration from real-world cultures, history, and scientific principles. Research can provide a solid foundation for believable world-building.

Reader/Viewer Engagement:
Leave room for exploration and imagination. Allow your audience to participate in discovering the world's intricacies rather than providing every detail upfront.

Incorporating these tools and techniques into your world-building process will help you create captivating and immersive settings that enhance your storytelling and captivate your audience. Remember that world-building is an ongoing process, evolving as your narrative unfolds.

Chapter 5: Blockchain Integration

Blockchain integration refers to the process of incorporating blockchain technology into existing systems, applications, or processes. It enables the seamless interaction of traditional systems with blockchain networks, allowing for the secure and transparent transfer of data or assets. This integration can have various purposes, such as enhancing transparency, security, and traceability in supply chains, financial transactions, healthcare records, and more. It often involves the use of smart contracts and APIs (Application Programming Interfaces) to connect and interact with blockchain networks like Ethereum or Hyperledger

NFTs and In-Game Assets

NFTs (Non-Fungible Tokens) and their integration into blockchain technology have revolutionized the world of in-game assets. These unique digital tokens have provided gamers and game developers with new opportunities and challenges, fundamentally altering how virtual items are owned, traded, and valued within video games.

Ownership and Provenance:
NFTs use blockchain technology to establish ownership and provenance of in-game assets.

Each NFT represents a unique digital item, such as skins, weapons, or virtual real estate. This ensures that players have true ownership of their in-game items, as the ownership records are stored on an immutable blockchain ledger. This prevents items from being duplicated or counterfeited.

Interoperability:

NFTs have the potential to be interoperable across multiple games and platforms. For example, a unique sword NFT acquired in one game could be used or traded in another compatible game.
This cross-game interoperability can create exciting new experiences for players and a

secondary market for in-game assets.

Player-driven Economies:

NFTs enable the emergence of player-driven economies within games. Players can buy, sell, and trade their digital assets with other players, potentially earning real-world value.

In the game Axie Infinity, players can breed and trade NFT creatures called Axies, turning the game into an income source for some players.

Scarcity and Rarity:

NFTs allow developers to create scarce in-game items. These limited-edition assets can become highly sought-after and valuable.

For instance, CryptoKitties introduced the concept of unique, breedable digital cats, with some selling for thousands of dollars due to their rarity.

Monetization for Developers: Game developers can benefit from NFT integration through new monetization strategies. They can sell NFTs directly to players, take a commission from in-game asset sales, or charge transaction fees on the blockchain.

NBA Top Shot, which sells officially licensed NBA highlights as NFTs, is an example of how this can work in practice.

Challenges and Concerns:

Energy consumption:

Some blockchain networks used for NFTs, like Ethereum, have faced criticism for their environmental impact due to high energy consumption.

Scalability:

Scalability issues can slow down or increase transaction costs on certain blockchains during times of high demand, impacting the usability of NFTs.

Regulatory concerns:

Governments are still developing regulations for NFTs, which could affect their legality and taxation. The integration of NFTs into gaming has transformed the industry by introducing true ownership, interoperability, and player-driven economies. While it presents exciting opportunities for gamers and developers, it also brings challenges that must be addressed for sustainable growth and adoption in the future.

Smart Contracts for Virtual Economies

In the world of blockchain technology, smart contracts have emerged as a transformative tool for automating and securing transactions. When applied to virtual economies, such as those found in online games or virtual reality environments, smart contracts offer numerous benefits and opportunities for innovation.

1. Digital Asset Ownership and Trading:

Smart contracts enable users to have true ownership of digital assets within virtual economies. For instance, in a blockchain-based game, players can own unique in-game items as non-fungible tokens (NFTs). These NFTs are controlled by smart contracts, ensuring that players have verifiable ownership and can trade them peer-to-peer.

2. Scarcity and Rarity:

Smart contracts can establish scarcity and rarity within virtual economies. Game developers can create limited-edition digital assets with programmed scarcity rules. For instance, only a specific number of legendary swords might exist in a game, creating demand among players and value in the virtual economy.

3. Secure Transactions:

Smart contracts eliminate the need for intermediaries, ensuring secure and transparent transactions. When a player purchases an in-game item from another player, the smart contract automatically transfers ownership and the corresponding digital currency, with all actions recorded on the blockchain.

4. Automated Rewards and Incentives:

Game developers can use smart contracts to automate rewards and incentives for players based on in-game achievements. For example, completing a difficult quest could trigger the smart contract to distribute unique tokens or in-game currency to the player's wallet.

5. Governance and Decision-Making:

In virtual economies with decentralized governance, smart contracts can facilitate community-driven decisions. Token holders can vote on changes to the virtual world's rules, and the smart contract can execute these decisions automatically.

6. Cross-Platform Compatibility:

Smart contracts can bridge virtual economies across different platforms or games. For example, a player might use a sword obtained in one blockchain-based game as a character's weapon in another, thanks to interoperable smart contracts.

7. Fraud Prevention:

By design, smart contracts are tamper-proof. This quality is especially valuable in virtual economies, where fraud and cheating can undermine fairness. Smart contracts ensure that the rules of the virtual world are upheld consistently.
You might gain more understanding from the following examples.

Example 1: Decentraland (MANA) and LAND:

Decentraland is a virtual world built on the Ethereum blockchain. In Decentraland, users can buy, sell, and build on parcels of virtual land, represented as NFTs called LAND. Smart contracts govern land ownership, allowing users to transfer and develop their parcels securely. This illustrates how blockchain integration and smart contracts enable unique virtual assets.

Example 2: CryptoKitties:

CryptoKitties, another Ethereum-based project, showcases how smart contracts can create digital collectibles with unique traits and limited supply. Each CryptoKitty is an NFT governed by smart contracts, and users can buy, breed, and trade them, demonstrating the fusion of virtual economies and blockchain technology.

Smart contracts have revolutionized virtual economies by providing trust, security, and automation. Their integration with blockchain technology has paved the way for novel experiences, digital asset ownership, and decentralized governance within virtual worlds. As technology continues to evolve, we can anticipate even more innovative applications in the ever-expanding landscape of virtual economies.

Decentralized Identity and Ownership

Decentralized identity and ownership, when integrated with blockchain technology, represent a transformative paradigm shift in how individuals and entities manage and assert control over their digital assets and personal information. This innovative approach offers increased security, privacy, and autonomy while reducing reliance on centralized authorities.

Self-Sovereign Identity (SSI)

Blockchain Integration:

Self-sovereign identity (SSI) leverages blockchain to provide individuals with full ownership and control over their digital identities. Instead of relying on centralized identity providers, users can create and manage their identities on a blockchain, granting or revoking access as needed.

For example, Sovrin, a decentralized identity network built on a permitted blockchain, enables users to manage and prove their identities without intermediaries.

Digital Ownership and NFTs (Non-Fungible Tokens)

Blockchain Integration:

NFTs are unique digital assets representing ownership of a specific item, artwork, or collectible. These tokens are recorded on a blockchain, providing immutable proof of ownership.

For example, CryptoKitties, one of the earliest NFT projects, allows users to buy, sell, and trade unique virtual cats, each represented by an NFT on the Ethereum blockchain.

Decentralized Finance (DeFi):

Blockchain Integration:

DeFi platforms are built on blockchain to provide users with decentralized control over their financial assets and services, eliminating the need for traditional financial intermediaries.

For example, Compound Finance, a DeFi lending and borrowing

protocol on Ethereum, allows users to earn interest or borrow assets directly from other users without intermediaries.
Data Ownership and Privacy:

Blockchain Integration:

Blockchain-based solutions enable individuals to control their data and grant access on a need-to-know basis. Users can monetize their data while maintaining privacy.
Example: Ocean Protocol is a decentralized data marketplace that empowers owners to share and monetize their data securely through blockchain technology.

Supply Chain and Provenance

Blockchain Integration:

Blockchain can be used to track the ownership and history of physical and digital assets in supply chains. This ensures transparency and trust in the origin and authenticity of products.

For example, IBM's Food Trust platform uses blockchain to trace the journey of food products from farm to table, enhancing food safety and supply chain efficiency.

Digital Rights Management (DRM):

Blockchain Integration:

Blockchain technology can be applied to DRM solutions to manage ownership and distribution of digital content, reducing piracy and ensuring fair compensation for creators.

for example, Verasity, a blockchain-based video platform, integrates blockchain to enhance content creators' control over their intellectual property and monetization.

Incorporating blockchain into decentralized identity and ownership systems empowers individuals, businesses, and organizations to exert greater control, security, and trust over their digital assets and personal information. These examples illustrate the diverse applications of blockchain technology in reshaping the way we manage and assert ownership in the digital age.

Chapter 6:
User Experience in the Metaverse

User Experience in the Metaverse" refers to the overall quality and satisfaction of users' interactions and engagements within virtual worlds or metaverse environments. It encompasses various aspects, including the ease of navigation, the realism and immersion of the virtual world, the quality of social interactions, and the accessibility of technology. A positive user experience in the metaverse aims to provide users with an enjoyable, intuitive, and meaningful interaction in these digital spaces. Designing for a good user experience in the metaverse is vital for its adoption and success.

User Onboarding and Tutorials

User onboarding and tutorials are crucial components of the user experience in the metaverse, as they play a significant role in helping individuals navigate and make the most of their virtual environments. In the metaverse, where the digital realm seamlessly blends with the physical world, it's essential to provide users with a smooth and informative introduction to this new reality. Here's an overview with examples and references:

Virtual Reality (VR) Headset Setup:

When a user first acquires a VR headset like the Oculus Quest or HTC Vive, the onboarding process often includes step-by-step tutorials to set up the hardware. These tutorials may use interactive 3D models and animations to guide users through the process. The Oculus Quest, for instance, has an intuitive setup wizard that includes clear visual instructions.
Avatar Creation:

In the metaverse, users typically create digital avatars to represent themselves. Providing intuitive and creative tools for avatar customization is essential. For

example, platforms like Roblox and Fortnite offer extensive avatar customization options, allowing users to express themselves in unique ways.
Navigation Tutorials:

Metaverse environments can be vast and complex. Tutorials can teach users how to navigate, teleport, or fly within the virtual world. For instance, in the VR game "Rec Room," there are interactive tutorial rooms where users can practice movement and interactions before exploring the main environment.
Social Interaction Guidance:

Since social interaction is a central aspect of the metaverse, tutorials can educate users on how to

communicate with others, send friend requests, and join virtual gatherings. Facebook Horizon, for instance, provides tutorials on gestures, emotes, and social interactions.
Economic Systems:

Some metaverse platforms incorporate virtual economies, where users can buy, sell, or trade digital assets. Tutorials are essential to explain these systems. Decentraland, a blockchain-based virtual world, offers tutorials on buying and owning virtual land and assets.
Content Creation and Building:

Metaverse users are often encouraged to create content. Tutorials can introduce users to

3D modeling, scripting, and world-building tools. Platforms like Roblox and Minecraft have extensive tutorials and communities to help users create their virtual worlds.
Privacy and Safety:

Tutorials should also cover privacy and safety guidelines. Users need to understand how to manage their digital presence and ensure a safe online experience. This is crucial, especially for younger users. Roblox, for instance, provides resources for parents and guardians to help them understand and control their children's online activities.
Progressive Onboarding:

As users gain experience, tutorials should adapt and offer more advanced topics. For example, in the VR platform AltspaceVR, users can start with basic tutorials and then progress to more complex events and interactions as they become more familiar with the environment.

In summary, user onboarding and tutorials in the metaverse are essential for creating a positive and engaging user experience. They guide users through the initial learning curve, empower them to express themselves and ensure their safety in this exciting new digital frontier. Successful metaverse platforms will continue to refine and expand their onboarding processes to cater to users of all ages and backgrounds.

Social Interaction and Networking

In the evolving landscape of the metaverse, social interaction and networking are pivotal aspects of the user experience, reshaping how people connect, collaborate, and build relationships in digital spaces. Here, I'll delve into the key elements and instances that define social interaction and networking within the metaverse:

Virtual Spaces as Meeting Grounds: Metaverse platforms offer diverse virtual spaces where users can meet, socialize, and interact. These spaces range from bustling cityscapes to serene natural environments, providing users with options for different types of gatherings. For example, users may gather in a virtual coffee shop for casual conversations or meet in a virtual conference room for professional discussions.

Avatars as Digital Representations: Users typically navigate the metaverse through avatars, which serve as their digital personas. These avatars can be customized extensively, allowing users to express their identity in creative ways. Users can modify their appearance, clothing, and even animations, enhancing self-expression in social interactions.

Immersive Communication: In the metaverse, communication transcends text and voice chat. Users can engage in spatial audio conversations, where proximity to others affects the volume and clarity of the conversation. This creates a more natural and immersive experience, akin to real-world interactions. Users can also use gestures, emotes, and non-verbal cues to express themselves.

Networking Opportunities: The metaverse offers unique networking opportunities, especially for professionals. Virtual conferences, trade shows, and workshops enable attendees to connect with peers and industry experts from around the world without the need for physical travel. Users can exchange virtual business cards, attend virtual job fairs, and even collaborate on projects within these spaces.

Content Creation and Sharing: Users can create and share content within the metaverse, further enriching their social interactions. This includes showcasing virtual art galleries, hosting live concerts, or sharing 3D models and designs. Social networks in the metaverse facilitate content discovery, allowing users to connect with creators who share their interests.

Cross-Platform Integration:

Many metaverse experiences are designed to be accessible across various platforms, from VR headsets to traditional desktop computers and mobile devices. This seamless integration ensures that users can engage with their social networks regardless of their preferred hardware, enhancing inclusivity and accessibility.

Privacy and Identity Management:

With the metaverse's extensive social features comes the importance of privacy and identity management. Users need robust tools to control who can access their personal information, interact with them, or join their virtual spaces. Balancing openness with user control is a critical aspect of metaverse design.

Virtual Economies and Social Capital:

The metaverse often incorporates virtual economies, where users can earn, spend, and trade digital assets. Social capital within the metaverse, such as reputation and influence, can also play a significant role in how users network and collaborate. For instance, a user with a strong virtual reputation may find it easier to attract collaborators or join exclusive communities.

Inclusivity and Diversity:

The metaverse's potential for inclusivity is a notable advantage. It can transcend physical limitations and foster diverse communities where users from different backgrounds come together. Developers and users alike emphasize the importance of creating welcoming spaces that promote diversity and inclusion.

In summary, social interaction and networking in the metaverse are redefining the way people connect and collaborate. With immersive experiences, customizable avatars, diverse virtual spaces, and innovative communication tools, the metaverse is poised to become a transformative platform for both personal and professional relationships. As it continues to evolve, addressing privacy concerns and promoting inclusivity will be crucial in shaping a positive and meaningful metaverse user experience.

Chapter 7: Metaverse Game Development Workflow

Agile Development in the Metaverse

Agile development in the metaverse is an innovative approach to creating digital experiences and applications within virtual worlds. This methodology adapts the principles of Agile software development to the unique challenges and opportunities presented by the metaverse, where users interact in immersive, interconnected virtual environments. Here, we'll delve into the key aspects of Agile development in the metaverse, along with relevant examples to illustrate its application.

Collaborative and Iterative Development:

Agile development in the metaverse emphasizes collaboration among multidisciplinary teams, just like traditional Agile methodologies. Developers, designers, and content creators work closely together to create and refine virtual experiences.
for instance, In building a metaverse-based virtual conference platform, the development team iteratively adds features based on user feedback. They start with a basic space and gradually incorporate features like

customizable avatars, interactive booths, and real-time chat, iterating after each sprint.

User-Centric Design:

User feedback is pivotal in the metaverse as it directly impacts the user's immersion and experience. Agile principles such as user stories and feedback loops help shape the development process.

For instance, a metaverse game studio collects player feedback on gameplay mechanics and level design through in-game surveys and social media. They prioritize and implement changes in response to player preferences and issues identified during gameplay.

Rapid Prototyping:

Metaverse projects often involve creating entirely new experiences. Agile encourages rapid prototyping, allowing developers to quickly test ideas and gather user feedback before committing to full-scale development.
For instance, A metaverse fashion startup uses rapid prototyping to create virtual clothing designs. They release a limited set of designs for user testing and iterate based on user preferences and feedback before producing a larger collection.
Flexibility and Adaptability:

The metaverse landscape is evolving rapidly, so Agile principles of adaptability and flexibility are crucial. Teams need to pivot and adjust to emerging technologies and trends.

Let's say, for instance, a metaverse education platform initially focused on virtual classrooms but quickly adapts to incorporate virtual field trips, based on the rising popularity of experiential learning in the metaverse.

Continuous Delivery and Updates:

Metaverse environments require constant maintenance and updates. Agile methodologies promote a continuous delivery approach, ensuring that new features and improvements are rolled out regularly.

for example, a metaverse social platform routinely releases

updates with new virtual world environments, social features, and user-generated content tools to keep users engaged and coming back for more.
Testing and Quality Assurance:

Agile development in the metaverse emphasizes rigorous testing to ensure a seamless user experience. Testing virtual environments requires a unique approach due to the immersive nature of the metaverse.
For example, a metaverse-based architectural visualization company conducts virtual walkthroughs of buildings to identify and rectify design flaws before the construction phase, improving the quality and efficiency of real-world projects.

In conclusion, Agile development in the metaverse empowers teams to create dynamic and engaging virtual experiences by adapting Agile principles to the unique challenges of this emerging digital frontier. The iterative, user-centric, and adaptable nature of Agile methodologies aligns perfectly with the demands of the metaverse, allowing developers and creators to stay at the forefront of this exciting technological landscape.

Collaborative Tools for Remote Teams

Collaborative tools for remote teams in metaverse game development have become essential in fostering efficient communication, coordination, and productivity among geographically dispersed team members. The metaverse game development industry presents unique challenges, such as the need for real-time collaboration on 3D assets, immersive environments, and complex game mechanics.

Here are some key collaborative tools and instances that illustrate their importance in this context:

Virtual Reality (VR) Meetings:

Teams can meet in virtual environments using VR headsets to discuss project progress. For example, a team working on a metaverse RPG might gather in a digital tavern to brainstorm quest ideas.

Benefits: VR meetings offer a more immersive and engaging way to interact, making it easier to visualize and iterate on game elements.

3D Modeling and Collaboration Platforms:

1. Platforms like Blender, Autodesk Maya, and Unity Collaborate allow artists and developers to work on 3D models simultaneously, even from different locations.

Benefits: Team members can collaborate on complex 3D assets in real-time, streamlining the design and development process.

Version Control Systems:

2. Tools like Git and SVN enable teams to track changes to the game's source code, scripts, and assets. This ensures that everyone is working with the latest versions. **Benefits:** Version control prevents conflicts, helps maintain a cohesive codebase, and allows for easy integration of new features.

Project Management and Communication Tools:

3. Platforms like JIRA, Trello, and Slack are used to track tasks, set deadlines, and facilitate communication among team members.

Benefits: These tools help keep the team organized, assign responsibilities, and ensure that everyone is on the same page regarding project goals and timelines.

In-Game Collaboration Features:

4. Some metaverse game engines, like Unreal Engine, offer collaborative editing features that allow multiple team members to work on the game world simultaneously.
Benefits: This feature accelerates level design and world-building, as developers, artists, and level designers can work together seamlessly within the game engine.

Cloud-Based Storage and File Sharing:

5. Services like Google Drive, Dropbox, and OneDrive provide a central location for storing and sharing project files, including game assets and documentation. **Benefits:** Cloud storage ensures that team members always have access to the latest project files, even when working remotely.

User Testing and Feedback Tools:

6. Platforms like TestFlight and PlaytestCloud allow remote playtesting of metaverse games, collecting valuable feedback from players worldwide.

Benefits: Developers can gather insights and make improvements based on user feedback, enhancing the overall gaming experience.

In conclusion, collaborative tools are the backbone of remote metaverse game development. They empower teams to work together efficiently, maintain quality, and bring immersive virtual worlds to life. These tools not only facilitate real-time collaboration but also enable geographically diverse talents to contribute their expertise seamlessly, pushing the boundaries of what metaverse games can offer.

Chapter 8:
Monetization Strategies

Monetization Strategies refer to the various methods and approaches game developers use to generate revenue from virtual worlds or metaverse environments. These strategies can include:

In-Game Purchases and Microtransactions

In the context of the metaverse, in-game purchases and microtransactions play a pivotal role in monetization strategies for developers and platform operators. These strategies have evolved significantly, reshaping the virtual economy within these expansive digital environments.

In-Game Purchases:

Virtual Goods and Assets: In-game purchases often revolve around the sale of virtual goods and assets, which can include anything from cosmetic items like skins, outfits, or weapon skins to functional items like power-ups or virtual real estate within the metaverse.

Scarcity and Exclusivity:
Developers create artificial scarcity by releasing limited edition or exclusive items, driving demand among players. Collectibles and rare items can

command high prices in the metaverse marketplace.

Customization and Personalization:

Players are drawn to the ability to customize their avatars or virtual spaces. In-game purchases offer a wide array of options, allowing users to express themselves uniquely within the metaverse.

Subscription Models:

Some metaverse platforms offer subscription-based services that grant access to premium content or exclusive perks. These subscriptions can provide a steady source of income for operators.

Microtransactions:

Small, Frequent Purchases: Microtransactions involve small, often inconspicuous purchases made within the game. These can include buying in-game currency, energy, or virtual items that enhance the gaming experience.

Loot Boxes and Gacha Systems:

Developers leverage chance-based mechanics like loot boxes and gacha systems to encourage microtransactions. Players spend money for a chance to obtain rare or desired items, fostering a sense of anticipation and excitement.

Energy and Time Accelerators: Microtransactions often include items that speed up

progress within the game. For example, purchasing energy or time accelerators can reduce wait times and allow players to achieve their goals faster.

Ad-Based Revenue:

Some metaverse experiences offer players the option to watch advertisements in exchange for in-game rewards or currency. This ad-based revenue model complements microtransactions.

Enhancing User Experience

Transparency and Fairness:

To maintain player trust, developers must be transparent about the odds of obtaining items through microtransactions and avoid creating a pay-to-win environment.

Balancing Free and Paid Content: Striking a balance between offering free content and incentivizing purchases is crucial. Players should be able to enjoy the metaverse without feeling pressured to spend money.

User Feedback and Iteration: Continuous feedback loops with the community help developers refine their monetization strategies. Listening to player concerns and adjusting pricing or mechanics accordingly can foster a healthier virtual economy.

Regulation and Ethics:

The increasing prevalence of in-game purchases and microtransactions has sparked discussions about regulation to protect consumers, particularly minors, from excessive spending.

In-game purchases and microtransactions are integral components of metaverse monetization strategies. When implemented thoughtfully, they can create sustainable revenue streams while enhancing the overall user experience. However, a delicate balance between profitability and player satisfaction is essential to ensure the long-term success of metaverse ecosystems.

Subscription Models

Subscription models have gained prominence in the metaverse as an alternative monetization strategy, providing a predictable and recurring income stream. Here are some key aspects to consider:

Tiered Subscriptions:

Metaverse platforms often offer tiered subscription plans. These plans can range from basic to premium, with each tier providing different benefits. For instance, a basic subscription might grant access to the metaverse, while a premium subscription could include exclusive virtual spaces, enhanced customization options, and a monthly allocation of in-game currency.

Exclusive Content:

Subscribers often enjoy access to exclusive content that non-subscribers cannot obtain. This content may include unique virtual items, experiences, or areas within the metaverse. These exclusives can incentivize players to subscribe, enhancing the perceived value of the subscription.

Steady Revenue:

Subscription models provide a steady and reliable source of income for platform operators and developers. This predictability can be advantageous for budgeting, planning updates, and maintaining servers and infrastructure.

Community Building:

Subscription-based communities often form around premium tiers. These communities may have dedicated forums, events, or in-game gatherings, fostering a sense of belonging among subscribers and enhancing player retention.

Free Trials:

Offering free trials of subscription services can be an effective way to attract new users. This allows players to experience the benefits of premium features before committing to a subscription.

Subscription Cancellation:

Developers must provide users with the option to cancel their subscriptions at any time. This user-friendly approach ensures that subscribers feel in control of their spending and can help maintain a positive reputation within the metaverse community.

Balancing Free and Paid:

Developers must strike a balance between providing meaningful benefits to subscribers and ensuring that non-subscribers can still enjoy the metaverse without feeling disadvantaged. This equilibrium is crucial for maintaining a healthy player base.

Feedback and Iteration:

Just like other monetization strategies, subscription models benefit from user feedback. Listening to subscribers' suggestions and concerns allows developers to refine their offerings, potentially leading to higher subscriber retention rates.

Cross-Promotions:

Partnerships between metaverse platforms and external brands or services can be used to enhance subscription models. For instance, offering discounts on real-world products or services to subscribers can add extra value to the subscription.

Subscription models are poised to play a significant role in the evolving metaverse landscape, offering an attractive option for players seeking premium experiences and for platform operators looking to establish stable financial foundations.

However, like all monetization strategies, their success ultimately depends on providing genuine value to users and maintaining a fair and enjoyable virtual environment.

Advertising and Sponsorship

Advertising and sponsorship are emerging as alternative revenue streams within the metaverse, offering unique opportunities for brands to engage with users while providing additional income for metaverse operators and developers.

In-World Advertising:

In the metaverse, advertising takes on a new dimension. Virtual billboards, banners, and even interactive ad spaces can be strategically placed within the digital environment. These in-world advertisements can be highly immersive and engaging, creating novel ways for brands to connect with their audience.

Personalized Advertising:

The metaverse's ability to gather user data and preferences can enable highly personalized advertising experiences. AI algorithms can analyze player behavior and serve ads that are more relevant to individual users, enhancing ad effectiveness.

Virtual Events and Experiences:

Brands can sponsor virtual events, concerts, or experiences within the metaverse. These sponsorships can include branded virtual spaces, exclusive in-game items, or even celebrity appearances, creating a strong connection between the brand and the metaverse community.

User-Generated Content (UGC):

UGC within the metaverse can also be sponsored. Brands can collaborate with content creators or encourage users to create content related to their products or services, fostering a deeper engagement with the brand.

Virtual Commerce:

Some metaverse platforms are experimenting with virtual commerce, where users can purchase real-world products through in-game stores or brand-sponsored spaces. This approach seamlessly integrates the virtual and physical worlds, offering convenience for users and new revenue streams for brands.

Economic Ecosystem: Advertising and sponsorship contribute to the metaverse's economic ecosystem by providing revenue that can be reinvested into platform development, infrastructure, and improvements, ultimately enhancing the user experience.

Ethical Considerations: As advertising becomes more integrated into the metaverse, ethical concerns arise, such as user privacy, data security, and the potential for intrusive ads. Striking a balance between monetization and user comfort is essential.

Regulation:

Governments and regulatory bodies are closely monitoring advertising practices in the metaverse, with an eye on protecting consumers from misleading or harmful ads. Operators and brands need to stay compliant with evolving regulations.

User Choice:

Metaverse operators should allow users to control their ad experience to a reasonable extent. This can include opt-in/opt-out features, ad frequency settings, and clear information about data collection and usage.

Advertising and sponsorship hold significant potential within the metaverse, creating a symbiotic relationship between brands, platform operators, and users. When executed thoughtfully and ethically, these strategies can contribute to the sustainability and growth of the metaverse ecosystem while offering unique and engaging experiences for users

www.ingramcontent.com/pod-product-compliance
Lightning Source LLC
Chambersburg PA
CBHW070951260726
48661CB00003B/1232